I'LL BE HOME
BEFORE
MIDNIGHT
AND I WON'T
GET
PREGNANT

I'LL BE HOME BEFORE MIDNIGHT AND I WON'T GET PREGNANT

STORIES OF ADOLESCENCE

BY
TONY WOLF

ILLUSTRATED BY
FRANCE MENK

Designed by Martin Moskof

VINTAGE BOOKS
A Division of Random House
New York

To Nick and Margaret.

To Liesel, Edi, Rachel, Josh, Nicky, and Willy.

A Vintage Original, May 1988
First Edition

Library of Congress Cataloging-in-Publication Data
Wolf, Tony.
I'll be home before midnight and I won't get pregnant.
1. Adolescence—Anecdotes, facetiae, satire, etc.
2. Youth—Attitudes—Anecdotes, facetiae, satire, etc.
3. Parenting—Anecdotes, facetiae, satire, etc.
4. Adolescent psychology—Anecdotes, facetiae, satire, etc.
I. Title.
HQ796.W63   1988   304.2'35   87-21670
ISBN 0-394-75566-9 (pbk.)

Manufactured in the United States of America
10 9 8 7 6 5 4 3 2 1

CONTENTS

INTRODUCTION

Parents seem to suffer an odd form of amnesia in dealing with their teenagers. Either they forget what it was like for themselves as teenagers, or they view their own adolescence through strangely colored glasses that blot out large parts of the way it actually was.

Teenagers are very much intent on their own concerns. Their focus is almost exclusively on what is happening in their personal world—which may be nothing more than lying in their room, rereading comic books, and listening to music. Anything a parent wishes to say is basically experienced by the teenager as a violent intrusion.

The problem is not even what parents say. It is that they exist, which is already more than most teenagers want to deal with. It is normal for teenagers to feel this way. It is not bad or good; it just is. It is part of normal development: the psychological necessity of a child, now almost adult, to pull away from his or her parents while still strongly emotionally tied to them.

As soon as children become teenagers, they develop an allergy to their parents. But parents seem to forget that they, too, had a similar allergy. So when their own children act toward them as if they, the parents, had some kind of loathsome, contagious disease and are beneath respect, the parents respond with outrage and hurt: "How can they say that to me?" "How can they treat me that way?" Have they forgotten?

It is true that times have changed in the sense that teenagers are more outspoken with adults than they used to be. They use language that parents would never have used with their parents. But the way most teen-agers feel has not changed. Parents of teenagers were afflicted with exactly the same allergy when they were young.

In their children's eyes, parents change from a love object to a burden. This is not fun for the parents, but that is how it is. It is hard not to take what a teenager says or does personally. "Why does she hate me?" "Where have I failed?" Yet to take it in a personal way really is to fail to see it for what it is. More often than not, teenagers react to their parents not for who they are, but purely as parents. It is useful for parents of teenagers to be able to see things in the bigger, longer-term picture. It is also useful to have a sense of humor.

Adolescence is a stage. It does pass, and views about things, especially one's parents, change with it. The child who absolutely cannot stand his or her parents, as an adult, more often than not, no longer hates them at all. Underneath the allergy the love is still there. It is just that during adolescence, it is precisely that love which makes the adolescent feel childish and dependent, and hence is completely unacceptable. Teenagers' feelings about many things will change. But when you are a teenager, there is no way you can know that. Nor can a teenager be convinced otherwise—but this is understandable. If deep in your heart you feel a particular way, why should you believe that at some later date you are not going to feel that way at all? An adult can tell a teenager what's going to happen, how he or she will feel later on. But if what he or she is saying directly contradicts the teenager's own experience, the adult commentary is just not going to be that useful. Once they become adolescents, children can no longer believe adults just because they are adults and supposedly know better.

Teenagers feel they have to judge for themselves. And they will.

What follows are stories about being a teenager, and about being a parent of a teenager. Each is based on a real dilemma of adolescence. The stories are supposed to be helpful, mainly by being specific about things that can happen during adolescence, by pointing out that they don't happen to just one person. Maybe things are happening not because you are doing something wrong, but because you're part of a larger thing—adolescence— that everyone has to deal with. Knowing this doesn't solve anything, but hopefully it can make adolescence a little easier to live through. Even if everything seems out of control, it's not actually because of anything you're doing wrong. Furthermore, there really isn't much you can do about it except survive.

I am a psychologist who sees adolescents. I also have two teenagers of my own. I was an adolescent. All of the above are probably why I wrote these stories.

THE
BOY
WHO
TRIED
DRUGS

THE BOY WHO TRIED DRUGS

Drugs are a real problem; but they are a complicated problem. Heroin is a drug. Alcohol is a drug. Marijuana is a drug. But they are very different in their effects, their addictiveness, their acceptability, and in who uses them.

A boy growing up in a wealthy neighborhood who smokes marijuana on weekends is not in the same situation as a ghetto teenager who smokes crack.

A teenager who knows that he has an easier chance to have a job, a career, a family, just like his own parents has a strong motivation to be careful about, if not to avoid, drugs: "I don't want to mess up my future." But a teenage boy who thinks he doesn't have much of a future is different. It is for this reason that kids who do poorly in school seem to be at more of a risk for heavy drug involvement in high school: they feel they don't have a whole lot to lose.

Drugs are a problem that is not going to go away. As long as drugs are available, some teenagers will try them. And some will have drug problems. This is unavoidable. What is the best thing to do for teenagers regarding drugs?

Make sure they have the most accurate and honest—believable—information available to them, which is usually not the case, and make drug programs available to teenagers who do have problems. Unfortunately, such programs do not exist in most communities.

ONE FRIDAY NIGHT RICHIE, BUZZ AND JERRY WENT TO A PARTY.

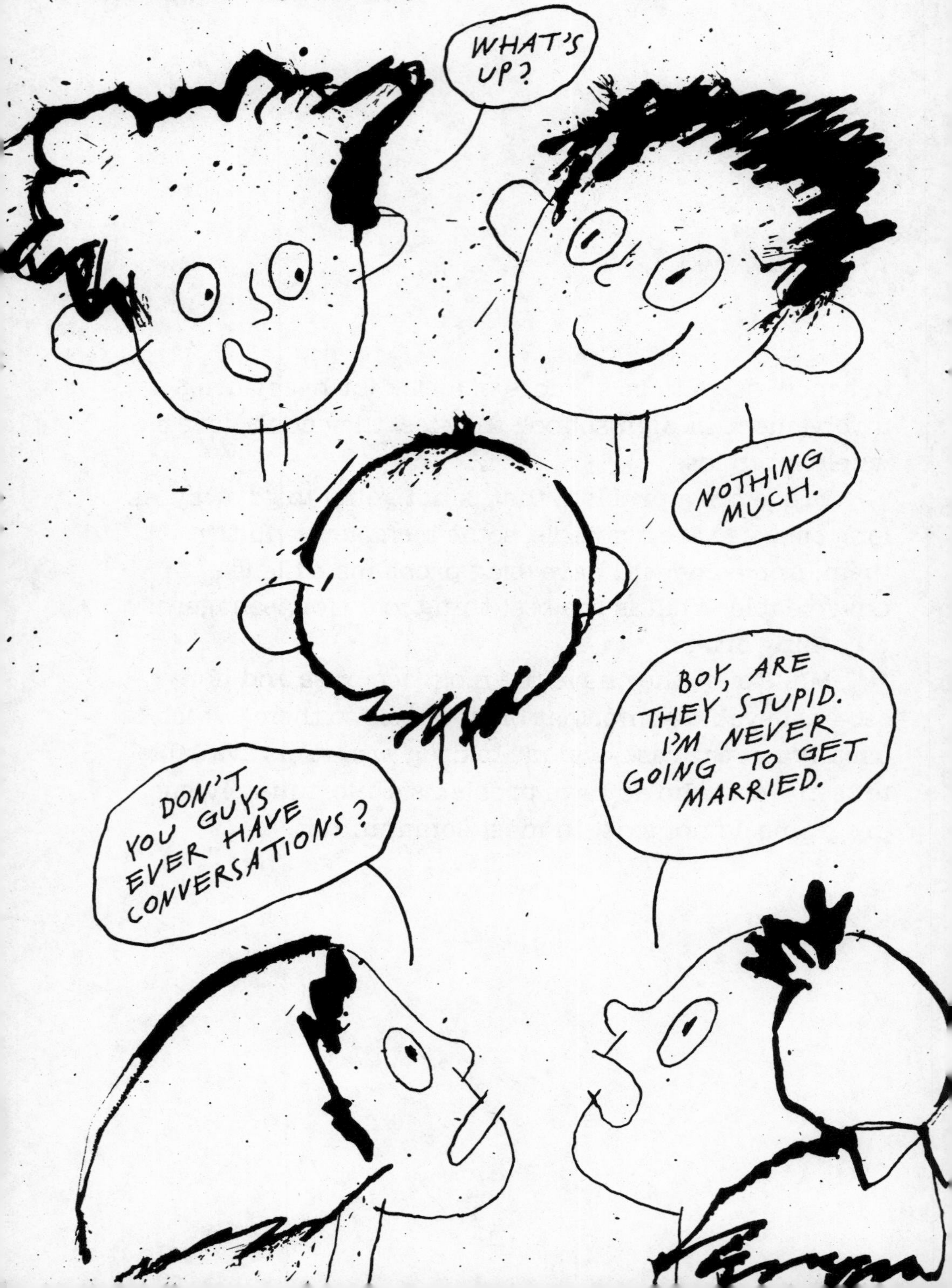

BUT A LITTLE LATER THAT EVENING JERRY
SAID TO RICHIE AND BUZZ:

RICHIE HAD NEVER HAD ANY KIND OF DRUGS
BEFORE. HE WAS A LITTLE AFRAID, BUT IT
SEEMED KIND OF EXCITING. HE HAD ALWAYS
THOUGHT HE WOULD PROBABLY TRY
MARIJUANA.

HE TRIED IT. AT FIRST HE DIDN'T FEEL ANY
DIFFERENT.

BUT AFTER A LITTLE WHILE, RICHIE DID FEEL DIFFERENT.

HE KIND OF LIKED IT. LATER HE WAS BACK TO NORMAL. HE FELT FINE. HE WENT HOME.

THE NEXT DAY RICHIE CHECKED HIMSELF OUT.

I SEEM FINE. I LIKED IT. IT WAS FUN. NO BIG DEAL.

BUT HE WASN'T SURE. RICHIE DECIDED TO TALK TO HIS PARENTS.

MOM, YESTERDAY I TRIED SOME DRUGS.

DON'T YOU HAVE ANY SENSE? DRUGS, ANY DRUGS, ARE DANGEROUS. I THOUGHT YOU HAD THE SENSE NOT TO TRY THEM. I'M VERY DISAPPOINTED. I DON'T KNOW WHAT TO SAY. I WILL HAVE TO TALK TO YOUR FATHER AND WE WILL HAVE TO DECIDE WHAT TO DO.

RICHIE DECIDED THAT MAYBE HIS PARENTS
WEREN'T GOING TO BE TOO HELPFUL AFTER
ALL.

HE REALLY DIDN'T KNOW WHERE TO GO TO
GET MORE INFORMATION.

I MEAN, I'M NOT WORRIED OR ANYTHING. BUT I MIGHT LIKE TO KNOW MORE. ALL I GOT IS WHAT THE OTHER KIDS SAY.

HE SMOKED MARIJUANA AGAIN. HE BEGAN TO SMOKE MOST WEEKENDS.

WHAT CAN I SAY? IT'S FUN.

MEANWHILE, RICHIE'S MOTHER COULDN'T STOP BEING SUSPICIOUS.

I THINK RICHIE MAY BE TAKING DRUGS.

I THINK YOU WORRY TOO MUCH, ETHEL.

BUT SHE WAS NOT REASSURED.

ONE DAY SHE DECIDED TO SEARCH RICHIE'S ROOM WHILE HE WAS AT SCHOOL.

BEHIND SOME SOCKS SHE FOUND SOME CIGARETTE PAPERS AND A SMALL PLASTIC BAG.

THAT NIGHT THERE WAS A GIANT SCENE.

RICHIE WAS GENUINELY UPSET. FINALLY, IN
TEARS, HE MADE UP A COUPLE OF LIES.

RICHIE'S PARENTS WERE NOT TOTALLY
CONVINCED.

RICHIE'S PARENTS DECIDED THAT THE ONLY SURE PLAN WAS TO LOCK HIM IN HIS ROOM AND BRING IN A TUTOR.

BUT AFTER TWO WEEKS, RICHIE TUNNELED OUT WITH A SCRAPER MADE WITH ALUMINUM FOIL FROM TV DINNERS.

NOT KNOWING WHAT ELSE TO DO, RICHIE'S PARENTS MORE OR LESS GAVE UP.

I KIND OF WISH THAT PSYCHOLOGIST FLY WAS BACK. HE SEEMED TO HAVE IDEAS.

OH SURE, NOW YOU'RE SORRY.

I DIDN'T SEE YOU STOPPING ME THEN.

MEANWHILE, BACK IN HIS NORMAL LIFE, RICHIE CONTINUED TO SMOKE MARIJUANA OCCASIONALLY.

I DON'T KNOW. IT SEEMS OKAY. I STILL CAN'T SEE ANY BAD EFFECTS.

BUT HE DECIDED TO TALK TO LES PULLMAN, WHO USED DRUGS BUT SEEMED TO BE A SENSIBLE GUY.

SHOULD I BE CAREFUL ABOUT ANYTHING?

DRUGS IN MODERATION ARE OKAY, BUT STAY AWAY FROM STRONG ADDICTING STUFF LIKE HEROIN AND CRACK.

BUT WHAT'S MODERATION? HOW CAN I KNOW IF I'M HOOKED ON SOMETHING?

USE YOUR JUDGMENT, MAN.

BUT RICHIE WAS NOT FULLY SATISFIED WITH LES' ANSWER.

SOME KIDS CAN HANDLE DRUGS, SOME KIDS CAN'T. BUT THEY ALL THINK THEY CAN.

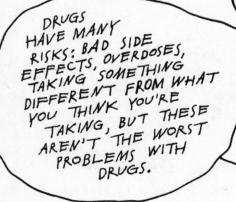

DRUGS HAVE MANY RISKS: BAD SIDE EFFECTS, OVERDOSES, TAKING SOMETHING DIFFERENT FROM WHAT YOU THINK YOU'RE TAKING, BUT THESE AREN'T THE WORST PROBLEMS WITH DRUGS.

WHAT'S THAT ON THE WALL?

I DUNNO. I THINK IT'S A FLY WITH THE HEAD OF A LADY PSYCHOLOGIST.

YOU KNOW, YOU REALLY ARE A JERK, YOU SQUISHED IT.

RICHIE DECIDED HE WASN'T GOING TO WORRY ANYMORE.

I'M SMOKING ALMOST EVERY WEEKEND AND NOTHING HAS HAPPENED TO ME. MAYBE SOME KIDS CAN'T HANDLE IT, BUT I CAN.

YOU MEAN THERE'S NOTHING WE CAN DO TO STOP HIM FROM TAKING DRUGS?

LIKE THE FLY SAID, IF THE DRUGS ARE THERE, KIDS ARE GOING TO USE THEM.

PARENTS ARE NOT TOTALLY HELPLESS. BY DISCUSSING DRUGS YOU DO INFLUENCE YOUR CHILD. IF YOU'RE REALLY CONCERNED, YOU SHOULD TRY TO GET MORE REALISTIC AND TRUTHFUL INFORMATION ABOUT DRUGS MADE AVAILABLE FOR BOTH YOU AND YOUR CHILDREN.

AND SO ACROSS AMERICA WORRIED BUT ALSO SADDENED PARENTS WATCHED AND SAID FAREWELL AS THEIR CHILDREN WENT OFF WITHOUT THEM INTO THE WORLD OF DRUGS. SOME WOULD STEER CLEAR OF TROUBLE, BUT SOME WOULD FOUNDER. BUT AS THEY ENTERED THIS NEW WORLD, ALL WOULD HAVE ONE THING IN COMMON: THEY WOULD ALL THINK THEY COULD HANDLE DRUGS.

MEANWHILE, THE PSYCHOLOGIST-FLIES HAD OVER-RUN A POWER STATION IN THE FIRST STEP OF THEIR PLAN TO TAKE OVER THE WORLD. BUT THAT'S ANOTHER STORY.

TED AND YVONNE

TED AND YVONNE

When some teenage girls fall in love, their love can be just as totally blind as anybody else's. This can be particularly trying to parents who discover that the power they have to do anything about this is absolutely zero. Also, not too infrequently, the boy in question may not be exactly what the parents had in mind for their daughter.

I'm not sure what I think about such early loves. Mainly they just are, despite what anybody thinks; I just hope they don't lead to early babies (which, unfortunately, they sometimes do). In the old days, people used to send their daughters to school in Europe for three years (in the days when they only had slow boats) or offer the undesirable boyfriend great sums of money to move to North Dakota (this does not work in North Dakota). These methods are still probably the only things that work.

In some ways I'm not sure if there is any love quite so total—to the extent that it fills up her whole life, *is* her whole life—as that of a teenage girl in love.

YVONNE WAS FIFTEEN.

YVONNE HAD ALWAYS LOVED STUFFED ANIMALS.
THEY WERE SO CUTE. SHE HAD ALWAYS
GOTTEN AS MANY OF THEM AS SHE COULD.
AND SHE LOVED THEM ALL.

YVONNE ALSO LIKED JEWELRY THAT HAD HEARTS ON IT. ACTUALLY, SHE JUST LIKED HEARTS IN GENERAL.

SHE DID NOT EXACTLY LIKE SCHOOL THAT MUCH, BUT SHE DID LIKE LUNCH PERIOD.

BEST OF EVERYTHING, YVONNE LIKED TO HANG OUT WITH HER FRIENDS, DONNA AND CHRISTEN.

YVONNE LOVED HER MOTHER AND FATHER, BUT SOMETIMES SHE DID GET INTO ARGUMENTS WITH THEM.

ALL IN ALL, YVONNE HAD A PRETTY NORMAL AND HAPPY LIFE. THEN ONE DAY YVONNE MET TED.

HE WAS A FRIEND OF DENISE'S EX-BOYFRIEND, ANTHONY. HE WAS KIND OF OLDER, AND HE WASN'T IN SCHOOL ANYMORE, AND HE WASN'T EXACTLY WORKING. BUT RIGHT AWAY, YVONNE LIKED HIM A LOT.

YVONNE AND TED STARTED GOING TOGETHER. AND AFTER A WHILE, YVONNE REALIZED THAT SHE WAS IN LOVE WITH TED.

SHE THOUGHT ABOUT HIM ALL THE TIME.
SHE WAS ONLY HAPPY WHEN SHE WAS WITH
HIM. YVONNE THOUGHT THAT TED WAS
TOTALLY WONDERFUL.

THEY HAD THEIR OWN SPECIAL SONG,
LOVE IS KINDA FUNNY, BY THE RUNNERS.

AND YVONNE ALWAYS GOT A SPECIAL
FEELING WHENEVER SHE HEARD IT.

SHE NOTICED THE RESEMBLANCE BETWEEN
TED AND GEORGE WASHINGTON.

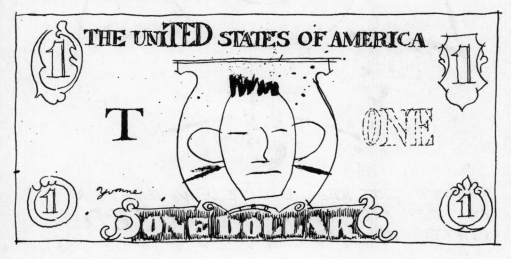

SHE VOTED FOR TED FOR HER CLASS PRESIDENT
EVEN THOUGH HE DIDN'T GO TO HER SCHOOL.

YVONNE RENAMED HER STUFFED ANIMALS.

YVONNE GOT REAL EXCITED WHENEVER
ANYBODY MENTIONED THE UNITED
STATES OF AMERICA.

YVONNE COULDN'T UNDERSTAND WHY TED HADN'T BEEN MADE PRESIDENT.

WHO ELSE COULD POSSIBLY BE BETTER?

YVONNE'S PARENTS, HOWEVER, WERE NOT SO THRILLED WITH TED.

YVONNE WAS TOTALLY HAPPY.

AND OF COURSE, SHE DID.

ON THEIR DATES THEY MAINLY SPENT
THEIR TIME IN TED'S CAR.

OR WATCHING TED WORK ON HIS CAR.

SOMETIMES TED WOULD BORROW THINGS
FROM YVONNE.

YVONNE, LEND ME TEN BUCKS, I NEED CIGARETTES.

WHICH HE NEVER SEEMED TO RETURN.

ALSO, AFTER A WHILE, TED DIDN'T SEEM TO
TALK TO YVONNE VERY MUCH.

GO IN THE HOUSE AND GET MY CIGARETTES.

EXCEPT WHEN HE WANTED SOMETHING.

ACTUALLY, TED DIDN'T SEEM TO PAY MUCH
ATTENTION TO YVONNE EXCEPT WHEN THEY
WERE IN THE CAR.

MAYBE
HE DOESN'T
LIKE MY
HAIR
COLOR.

YVONNE BEGAN TO HAVE DOUBTS ABOUT
HERSELF.

BUT SHE HAD NO DOUBTS ABOUT TED.

THOUGH HE SURE DID SEEM TO WANT A LOT OF STUFF.

YVONNE'S FRIENDS BEGAN TO TALK TO HER ABOUT TED.

EVEN HER PARENTS HAD DOUBTS.

BUT YVONNE WAS STILL CERTAIN.

HE'S MY DREAMBOAT.

THOUGH HE IS KIND OF NASTY SOMETIMES.

AND SHE NOTICED THEY WEREN'T PLAYING HER AND TED'S SONG ON THE RADIO SO MUCH ANYMORE.

THEN ONE DAY WHEN YVONNE WAS IN THE CAR WITH HER MOTHER, YVONNE NOTICED TED WITH ANOTHER GIRL.

LATER YVONNE ASKED TED ABOUT THE GIRL.

WHO WAS THAT GIRL YOU WERE WITH?

THAT WAS MY SISTER.

BUT TED DIDN'T HAVE A SISTER.

BUT YOU DON'T HAVE A SISTER.

SO? CAN YOU LEND ME TWENTY BUCKS?

SOON THEIR DATES STARTED TO BE DIFFERENT. TED MADE YVONNE RIDE IN THE TRUNK.

I LIKED IT BETTER WHEN I GOT TO BE IN THE FRONT PART.

YVONNE'S FRIENDS BECAME EVEN MORE OUTSPOKEN:

YOU'RE A FOOL, YVONNE.

HE'S TREATING YOU LIKE DIRT.

YVONNE DID BEGIN TO WORRY. A LITTLE.
SHE DECIDED TO CHECK OUT THE
"LETTERS TO DOROTHY DRAPER" COLUMN TO SEE
IF THERE WAS ANYTHING HELPFUL.

BUT THERE WAS ONLY ADVICE TO A LADY WHO
HAD LOST HER CAT.

THINGS GOT WORSE AND YVONNE BEGAN TO
FEEL REALLY TERRIBLE.

HE DID TREAT HER VERY BADLY.

THEN ONE DAY THERE WAS SOMETHING HELPFUL IN DOROTHY DRAPER.

THERE WAS A LETTER TO DOROTHY FROM A GIRL NAMED SYLVIA WHOSE PROBLEM WAS JUST LIKE HERS WITH TED. DOROTHY DRAPER ANSWERED:

DEAR SYLVIA, DON'T BE SUCH A BONEHEAD. HE'S A CREEP. DROP HIM LIKE YOU WOULD ANYTHING THAT'S ROTTEN AND SLIMY.

THAT DID IT.

DOROTHY IS RIGHT. I REALLY HAVE TO BREAK UP WITH TED.

THE NEXT DAY, YVONNE CONFRONTED TED.

TED, I HAVE SOMETHING TO SAY.

SHE TOLD HIM.
TED DIDN'T EVEN NOTICE.

BUT YVONNE NEVER DATED TED AGAIN.

YVONNE WENT ON, GOT MARRIED, GOT A JOB, HAD KIDS OF HER OWN, AND HAD A PRETTY FULL LIFE.

ALL IN ALL, SHE WAS HAPPY.

BUT THROUGHOUT HER LIFE, WHENEVER SHE WOULD ACCIDENTALLY SEE TED, OR HEAR OF HIM, OR ESPECIALLY WHEN SHE WOULD HEAR "LOVE IS KINDA FUNNY" ON AN OLDIES PROGRAM... YVONNE WOULD GET TO FEELING ALL SOFT INSIDE, AND SHE WOULD REMEMBER TED. NOT THE BAD TIMES. BUT HOW WONDERFUL HE HAD BEEN AND HOW MUCH SHE HAD LOVED HIM.

THE BOY WHO HAD SEXUAL FEELINGS

THE BOY WHO
HAD SEXUAL FEELINGS

I don't know if it's possible to understand what sex is like for a teenage boy unless you've been one. For teenage boys, sex more or less didn't exist before. Baseball games, candy, good TV shows really were way ahead of sex in interest. But once a boy is a teenager, sex is everywhere, all the time. It's in the air. Sex comes from way out left field to give everything a whole new coloring, and the coloring seems attached to one's penis.

Even for boys who are not experiencing their sexuality all of the time, that's what they're doing—*not* experiencing their sexuality all of the time, like a boy who's *really* into studying or *really* into sleeping.

The whole business can actually be fun if it's not too fraught with worry. "Am I normal?" "Am I man enough?" "Why aren't I having sex and everybody else is?" "They say masturbating is okay, but is it really?" "Will I actually be able to stop myself from reaching out and touching Rosa Winkleman's breasts tomorrow in social studies?"

ARNOLD HAD ALWAYS BEEN A PRETTY
REGULAR KID.

WHEN HE HAD BEEN IN GRADE SCHOOL, HE
LIKED MOST OF THE SAME STUFF AS OTHER
KIDS:

HE LIKED TO THINK OF HIMSELF AS SOMEBODY
WHO WAS NOTHING SPECIAL.

EVEN IN HIS FANTASIES.

HIS PARENTS WERE PROUD OF HIM.

HE WAS HAPPY AND HE WAS NORMAL.

ARNOLD KNEW ABOUT SEX, BUT THERE WAS OTHER STUFF THAT WAS A LOT MORE INTERESTING.

HE HAD SEEN PICTURES OF NAKED WOMEN.

DESIRE

YEAH,
THEY'RE
EXCITING.
WHEN'S
LUNCH?

AND HE LIKED THEM. SORT OF. THE TRUTH WAS,
SEX WASN'T THAT MUCH IN HIS MIND.

WHY DO I ALWAYS
GET THE FATTY PIECES
IN MY CHICKEN SALAD
SANDWICHES?

BUT THEN ONE DAY EVERYTHING
CHANGED. ARNOLD STARTED TO
NOTICE THINGS...

LIKE
BREASTS.

IN FACT, HE NOTICED THEM A LOT.

HE STARTED TO NOTICE OTHER THINGS. AND HE STARTED TO HAVE ALL KINDS OF NEW FEELINGS.

ALSO HE TOTALLY LOST CONTROL OF HIS PENIS.

ARNOLD THOUGHT ABOUT SEX ALL OF THE TIME.

I WONDER HOW MUCH GEORGE AND MARTHA WASHINGTON DID IT?

IN FACT, SEX SEEMED TO TAKE OVER HIS WHOLE WORLD. EVERYWHERE. ALL OF THE TIME. IN SCHOOL:

WILL MISS CHARNOWSKI'S BREASTS PLEASE COME TO THE OFFICE?

IN THE NEWSPAPERS:

THE DAILY BREAST

JUNE 4, 1984

PRESIDENT LEAVES FOR VAGINAL CONFERENCE

IN HIS SOUP:

HIS COUSIN STEPHANIE:

HIS COUSIN RACHEL:

HIS HOMEWORK:

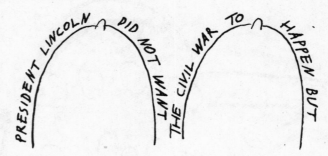

WHICH BECAME IMPOSSIBLE TO DO.

IN FACT, THE ONLY BOOKS HE WAS INTERESTED
IN WERE GIRLIE MAGAZINES AND <u>THE</u>
<u>WORLD BOOK OF SEXUAL RECORDS.</u>

THOUGH HAVING A
PENIS ONLY TWO INCHES
WHEN ERECT, CARLOS
GARCIA HOLDS THE
WORLD RECORD OF
BRINGING SEVENTEEN
DIFFERENT WOMEN
TO ORGASM WITHIN A
TWO-HOUR PERIOD.

WOW!

HE EVEN HAD TO GO TO A NEW CLOTHING
STORE.

CERTAIN PLACES HE FOUND TO BE SIMPLY TOO OVERWHELMING — LIKE DOWNTOWN.

ALSO HE FOUND CERTAIN NEWS ARTICLES DISTURBING.

THERE WAS NO TIME OR PLACE THAT THE SEX THOUGHTS EVER LEFT HIM ALONE.

GIANT BREASTS TRIED TO GET IN HIS WINDOW AT NIGHT.

ARNOLD BEGAN TO FEAR THAT HIS SEXUALITY WOULD GET COMPLETELY OUT OF CONTROL.

BOY JAILED FOR SEXUAL ATTACK ON FURNITURE

HE FELT THAT HIS SEXUALITY KNEW NO BOUNDS.

ARNOLD WAS AFRAID THAT HE HAD BECOME A SEX MANIAC.

ARNOLD DECIDED TO STOP THINKING ALTOGETHER.

THIS DIDN'T WORK TOO WELL.

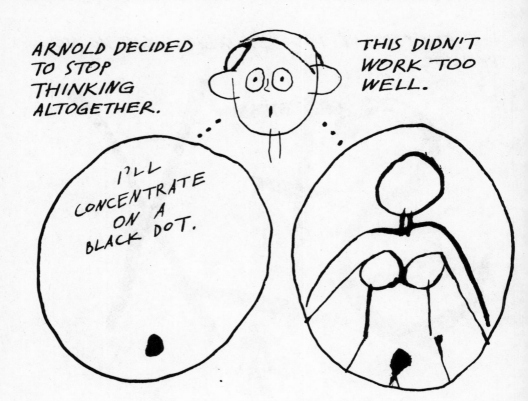

IN DESPERATION, HE TURNED TO HIS FRIEND DWAYNE, WHO IT TURNED OUT HAD SIMILAR PROBLEMS... AND WHO HAD A HELPFUL SUGGESTION.

THE SUGGESTION DIDN'T WORK, BUT ARNOLD
WAS HAPPY TO HAVE SOMEONE WHO
SHARED HIS INTERESTS.

I HEARD THAT ROGER FELTON, THAT KID WHO'S A PHYSICS GENIUS, MADE A FOUR-FOOT-HIGH VAGINA THAT HE KEEPS IN HIS ROOM.

IN FACT, ANOTHER FRIEND, RICHARD, WHO
ARNOLD DISCOVERED ALSO SHARED HIS
DISABILITY, ACTUALLY SOMEHOW GOT HOLD
OF AN ILLUSTRATED COPY OF THE
INFAMOUS PATHOGENICA GENITALICUS,
THE BOOK ON DISEASES AND DEFORMITIES
OF THE PENIS...

INCREDIBLY GROSS!

AWESOME!

VERY BIG!

PATHOGENICA GENITALICUS

... INCLUDING THE LEGENDARY
NYSTRIM'S SYNDROME, AS A RESULT OF
WHICH THE MALE GENITALS GROW TO
THE SIZE OF A SMALL HORSE.

IT WAS ALSO UNDER THE URGING OF HIS TWO
FRIENDS THAT ARNOLD RESPONDED TO AN
AD ON THE BACK OF A COMIC BOOK.

THE
ESSENCE
OF ALL
SEX

ONLY THE BRAVE
DARE SEND FOR
THIS OFFER.

SEND $20.00 TO:
SLIMY EDDIE
BOX 3601
PILTON, ILLINOIS

THE PARCEL ARRIVED TWO WEEKS LATER.

BUT UNFORTUNATELY IT WAS INTERCEPTED
BY ARNOLD'S MOTHER ... WHO, SENSING ITS
CONTENTS, HAD ARNOLD'S FATHER DESTROY
IT IN THE BACKYARD.

A FEW DAYS LATER, THERE WAS AN INCIDENT
AT SCHOOL.

ARNOLD WAS SITTING AT A LUNCH TABLE
WHEN DONNA CHAMBERS DROPPED A FORK
NEAR WHERE ARNOLD WAS SITTING. IN
PICKING UP THE FORK, ONE OF HER
BREASTS ACCIDENTALLY RUBBED AGAINST
ARNOLD'S BACK... AND ARNOLD FAINTED.

ARNOLD'S FRIENDS THOUGHT MAYBE HE
SHOULD START DATING. HE ASKED OUT
GRETCHEN SCHUSTER.

UNFORTUNATELY, ONCE ON THE DATE, ARNOLD
BECAME TOTALLY PARALYZED, AND HE HAD TO
BE CARRIED TO A HOSPITAL ON A STRETCHER.

THE PARALYSIS WORE OFF RATHER QUICKLY.

ARNOLD TRIED AGAIN AND ASKED OUT NAOMI CARDIGAN. ON THIS DATE, UNACCOUNTABLY, ARNOLD COULD DO NOTHING BUT RECITE EARLY SPEECHES OF WINSTON CHURCHILL.

FINALLY, HE TRIED LINDA WIZNER... AND ON THE DATE THEY GOT ON FINE. UNFORTUNATELY,

WHAT ARE YOU GOING TO DO WHEN YOU'RE OLDER?

I'M BECOMING A NUN TOMORROW.

ARNOLD DECIDED TO GIVE UP ON DATING.

THIS IS RIDICULOUS. I DON'T HAVE TO BE A SLAVE TO MY DESIRES.

HE DISCOVERED A BOOK.

MIND OVER

LUST

SUCCESS IN LIFE
AND REAL ESTATE
INVESTING THROUGH
CONTROLLED THINKING.

BY ARTHUR TINKHAM

AIDED BY THE WISDOM OF THE BOOK, ARNOLD BEGAN A NEW CAMPAIGN.

REALLY, IT'S JUST A MATTER OF WILL POWER. I CAN SIMPLY OVERPOWER MY SEXUAL DESIRES.

AND DURING THE DAYTIME IT SEEMED TO WORK, SORT OF.

UNFORTUNATELY, AT NIGHT IT WAS A
DISASTER. THE BREASTS ATTACKED IN LEGION.

IT SEEMED HIS SEXUALITY WAS JUST TOO POWERFUL.

TO MAKE MATTERS WORSE, ARNOLD HEARD IN SCHOOL THAT HIS FRIEND DWAYNE HAD BEEN SENT AWAY BY HIS PARENTS TO THE INSTITUTE FOR THE SEXUALLY DEPRAVED.

ARNOLD FELT THAT IT WAS NOW ONLY A MATTER OF TIME.

AND THE NEXT DAY, ALL OF HIS FEARS WERE
REALIZED.

ARNOLD'S TOWN, IN ITS PERIODIC SWEEP TO
RID ITSELF OF THE SEXUALLY CONSUMED,
WAS GOING TO CHECK OUT EVERY BOY AT
ARNOLD'S HIGH SCHOOL. AND TO DO THIS
THEY WERE BRINGING IN AN SV-17.

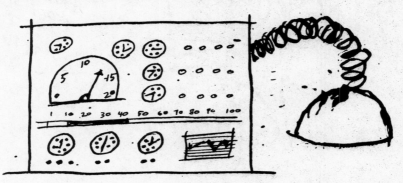

THE SV-17 WAS A HIGHLY SOPHISTICATED
PIECE OF ELECTRONIC EQUIPMENT THAT
MEASURED LEVELS OF SEXUAL THOUGHTS AND
URGES.

THE SCALE WENT FROM **0** TO **100**. ANYBODY
WHO SCORED OVER **40** WOULD BE
CONSIDERED SEXUALLY DEPRAVED AND
SENT AWAY.

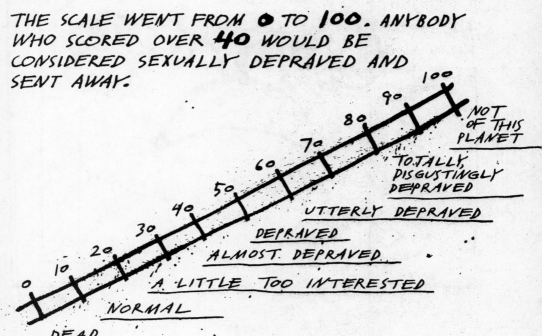

NOT OF THIS PLANET

TOTALLY, DISGUSTINGLY DEPRAVED

UTTERLY DEPRAVED

DEPRAVED

ALMOST DEPRAVED

A LITTLE TOO INTERESTED

NORMAL

DEAD

THE VERY NEXT DAY THE TESTING BEGAN.
ARNOLD WAS CALLED OUT OF THIRD PERIOD
FOR HIS TEST.

THEY HOOKED HIM UP TO THE SV-17.

THEY DID NOT TELL HIM
HOW HE HAD DONE, BUT
ARNOLD HAD SEEN QUITE
CLEARLY THAT HE HAD
REGISTERED AN 81.

NOT OF
THIS PLANET

TOTALLY
DISGUSTINGLY
DEPRAVED

80

THOUGH HE EXPECTED TO
BE TAKEN AWAY AT ANY
MOMENT, THE DAY WENT
BY AND NOTHING
HAPPENED.

MAYBE
THE
INSTITUTE
BUS BROKE
DOWN.

NOTHING HAPPENED THE
NEXT DAY, OR THE DAY
AFTER THAT.

I WONDER
WHAT'S
GOING
ON ?

NOBODY WAS TAKEN AWAY.

THEN GRADUALLY, A RUMOR BEGAN TO
CIRCULATE, WHICH WAS CONFIRMED WHEN
ANDY LEFTNER STOLE A COPY OF THE TEST
RESULTS FROM THE OFFICE.

EVERY BOY IN THE WHOLE SCHOOL HAD
SCORED WAY OVER 40 ON THE TEST,
EXCEPT FOR LARRY NIEDLER, WHO GOT
A 13,

WHO WAS SENIOR CLASS PRESIDENT.

ARNOLD— AND A LOT OF OTHER BOYS—
WERE VERY RELIEVED.

I GUESS I'M A
SEX MANIAC, BUT I MUST
BE A NORMAL ONE.

ARNOLD'S SEX MANIA DID NOT GO AWAY.

I WONDER
IF THERE HAVE
EVER BEEN
WOMEN WITH
THREE
BREASTS?

BUT HE DID DISCOVER SOMETHING THAT ACTUALLY HELPED. HE WENT OUT FOR THE CROSS-COUNTRY TEAM. AND HE RAN EVERY DAY.

A LONG DISTANCE, LIKE 20 MILES.

AND HE WAS VERY TIRED AT NIGHT.

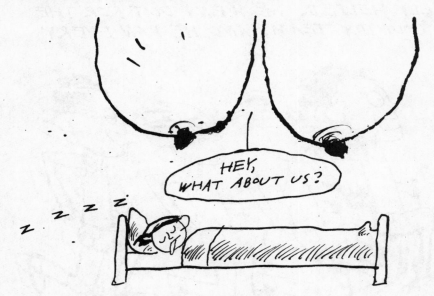

HEY, WHAT ABOUT US?

IN FACT, ARNOLD SURVIVED INTO HIS SENIOR YEAR IN HIGH SCHOOL, WHEN HE MET RACHEL PILSNER, WHO WAS ALSO A SENIOR AND WAS IN HIS CHEMISTRY CLASS.

RACHEL WAS REAL NICE, AND ARNOLD LIKED HER A LOT, AND THEY BEGAN TO DATE.

AND AFTER A WHILE THEY ACTUALLY DID SEXUAL THINGS AND ARNOLD LIKED IT A LOT.

ARNOLD WAS HAPPY.

OF COURSE THE BREASTS STILL VISITED ARNOLD AT NIGHT.

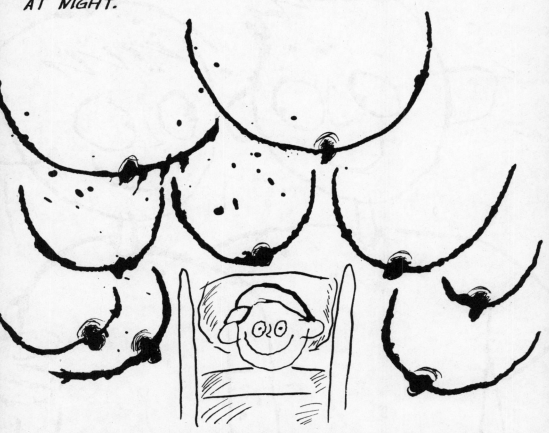

BUT AT LEAST THEY WERE RACHEL'S BREASTS AND MAYBE IF HER PARENTS WEREN'T HOME THURSDAY AFTER SCHOOL, HE'D HAVE A SHOT AT THEM.

WENDY'S HAPPY DREAM

A STORY OF TEENAGE PARENTS

WENDY'S HAPPY DREAM—
A Story of Teenage Parents

There are about sixty good reasons why it is not a good idea for people to have children when they are in their teens. Teenage mothers care more about having a good time (which is what teenagers are, appropriately, supposed to care about) than about being mothers. Being a mother is very demanding. Unless one has a convenient grandmother who will take on the main burden of child care, a teenage mother more often than not is going to resent the extraordinary—and totally normal—time demands of her baby. Forget about teenage fathers. Most regular fathers don't participate in early child care, let alone less mature teenage fathers, who invariably did not want to have the baby to begin with. That is, if the fathers are still around; in the large majority of teenage relationships, they aren't. That leaves the mothers to raise the child(ren) alone.

This may not ruin the lives of the teenage parents. Mainly it deprives them of the fun of young adulthood: of being independent, having money, actually being able to do things that they want to do. For both men and women, the main problem is probably financial. Instead of being able to work and save money, the young parents are immediately saddled with the cost of children and are doomed to be a whole lot poorer than they would have been if they had not had kids so early.

My main concern is not for the parents. Their lives are hurt, but probably not ruined. My concern is for the children. For all of the above reasons and more, teenage parents, teenage mothers—since, as stated, the fathers usually are not a significant part of the picture—simply do not have the patience and maturity to be good parents. Teenage parents make lousy parents. The same woman who, six years later at twenty-two, will be a good parent, at sixteen is still too much caught up in herself, in her own needs, to have the patience to be a good mother. As a result, the kids of such women do grow up to be more screwed up than other kids. All too frequently they become teenage parents themselves. Teenage parenting is an awfully easy way to pass on, generation to generation, a pretty lousy existence.

CARL AND WENDY WERE GOING TOGETHER
IN HIGH SCHOOL.

THEY OFTEN HAD SEX, BUT THEY KNEW WENDY
WOULDN'T GET PREGNANT.

THEY WERE PRETTY HAPPY.

THEN ONE NIGHT WENDY HAD A DREAM.

IN THE DREAM WENDY FOUND OUT THAT SHE WAS PREGNANT.

NO QUESTION ABOUT IT. YOU'RE PREGNANT.

IN THE DREAM SHE TOLD CARL.

GUESS WHAT, CARL?

YOU AND ME, WE'RE NUMERO UNO COUPLE.

WELL, YES THAT. BUT ALSO, I'M PREGNANT.

CARL WAS SURPRISED.

GOLLY GOSH, SILLY US, I GUESS YOU COULD GET PREGNANT.

CARL AND WENDY WERE BOTH PLEASED AS PUNCH.

IN THE DREAM, WENDY AND CARL TOLD THEIR PARENTS. THEY WERE PLEASED AS PUNCH TOO.

IN THE DREAM, THEY GOT MARRIED AND A
WEEK LATER BABY JERRY WAS BORN.

WENDY AND CARL WERE THRILLED WITH
BABY JERRY.

THEY SURE DID LOVE HIM.

THEY MOVED INTO THEIR VERY OWN PLACE
IN A ROOM OVER WENDY'S PARENTS' GARAGE.

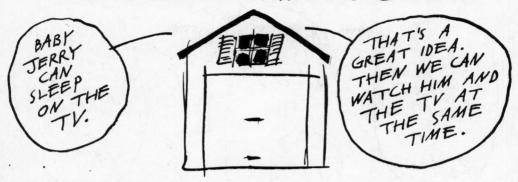

WHENEVER BABY JERRY WANTED TO BE FED,
THEY JUST GAVE HIM A BOTTLE.

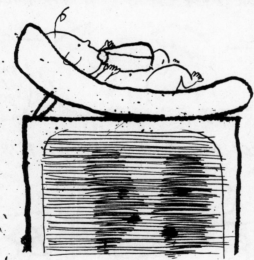

THEY DIDN'T MIND THAT BABY JERRY CRIED
A LOT.

IN THE DREAM, BABY JERRY NEVER TIED THEM DOWN.

OR THEY TOOK BABY JERRY WITH THEM.

THEIR FRIENDS WERE ALWAYS AT BURGER BOY.

THEY WEREN'T WORRIED.

SURE ENOUGH, THERE HE WAS, IN THE CAR.

BABY JERRY NEVER GOT IN THE WAY OF CARL
AND WENDY'S FUN.

THEIR LIFE AT HOME WITH BABY JERRY WAS
JUST GREAT. IN THE DREAM, WENDY DIDN'T
MIND IT AT ALL THAT CARL NEVER HELPED
WITH BABY JERRY.

IN THE DREAM, WENDY DIDN'T MIND IT THAT
CARL LEFT HER AT HOME A LOT.

SHE NEVER FELT TRAPPED BY BABY JERRY, OR
THAT EVERYTHING WAS GOING ON WITHOUT
HER, THAT BABY JERRY WAS AN INTOLERABLE
BURDEN, THAT THE WALLS WERE CLOSING IN
ON HER.

THEY SURE HAD HAPPY TIMES WITH BABY JERRY.

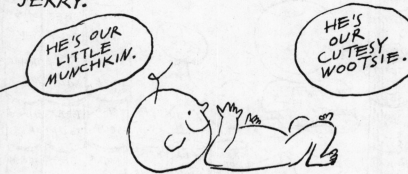

IN THE DREAM WENDY AND CARL GRADUATED FROM HIGH SCHOOL.

THEN THEY BOTH GOT JOBS WORKING IN THE LOCAL SUPERMARKET.

BABY JERRY LOVED THE SUPERMARKET.

AND SO DID HIS NEW SISTER, BABY JENNY.

IN THE DREAM, BABY JERRY DIDN'T EVEN MIND IT WHEN, A YEAR LATER, THEIR MARRIAGE FELL APART, AND WENDY AND CARL GOT DIVORCED.

AFTER ALL, HE WAS ONLY TWO AND A HALF, WHAT DID HE KNOW?

AT THAT POINT, WENDY WOKE UP.

AND WOULDN'T YOU KNOW IT, THE DREAM CAME TRUE, SORT OF.

JUST LIKE THE DREAM, WENDY FOUND OUT SHE WAS PREGNANT.

BUT WHAT HAPPENED NEXT WASN'T QUITE LIKE THE DREAM AT ALL.

AND WHAT FOLLOWED NEXT WASN'T LIKE
THE DREAM EITHER, AND MOST OF IT
WAS BAD. ONLY THE END WAS THE SAME.

DEBBY
AND.
HER
FRIENDS

DEBBY AND HER FRIENDS

Young teenage girls can be extraordinary cruel, especially to one another. The word *clique*, as in "we are a special group whose main pleasure is in making it clear that you are not part of it," is defined by the behavior of sixth-, seventh-, and eighth-grade girls. By high school the cliques usually break down or at least lose much of their meaningfulness and meanness. Yet, through the middle school years, they have a terrific power for those both in and outside of them.

There is a desperation to it all. It is so important for young teenage girls to be part of, and liked by, a group of friends. They constantly jockey for position for fear that they might be left out. Tina to Gretchen: "Rebecca said to me that she didn't like your bracelet. Don't you think she's stuck up?" Tina actually likes Rebecca, but for no particular reason she is so insecure that she wants to shore up her bond with Gretchen.

This doesn't happen so much with boys because they tend to fight. Also they don't talk to one another so much about relationships.

Even genuinely nice girls are capable of being incredibly cruel to one another at this age. Usually they grow out of it. But sixth through eighth grades can be a real social meat grinder. There are many girls who get ground up and never quite recover.

DEBBY HAD TWO GOOD FRIENDS: KARYN AND BIANCA.

AND AT SCHOOL, DURING LUNCH, THEY ALWAYS SAT TOGETHER.

RACHEL USUALLY SAT WITH THEM, BUT SHE WASN'T QUITE AS GOOD A FRIEND.

AT NIGHT THE FOUR OF THEM TALKED TO ONE ANOTHER ON THE PHONE A LOT.

TALKING ON THE PHONE MADE DEBBY FEEL GOOD. AND SAFE.

BEST OF ALL, DEBBY LIKED IT WHEN SHE AND KARYN AND BIANCA WERE DOING STUFF TOGETHER— LIKE GOING TO THE MALL.

ACTUALLY, DEBBY LIKED IT A LOT WHEN SHE
AND KARYN AND BIANCA WERE SAYING
BAD THINGS ABOUT OTHER KIDS. IT MADE
HER FEEL SUPERIOR.

DEBBY AND HER FRIENDS COULD GET
PRETTY MEAN.

FOR EXAMPLE:

THERE WAS A GIRL IN THEIR CLASS NAMED
TRUDY BACON WHO WASN'T EXACTLY A
COMPLETE LOSER.

BUT SHE WASN'T VERY SELF-CONFIDENT.

ONE DAY AT SCHOOL DEBBY AND HER
FRIENDS DECIDED TO HAVE A TALK
WITH TRUDY TO HELP HER.

TRUDY WAS EXCITED THAT A GROUP LIKE
DEBBY AND HER FRIENDS WANTED TO
TALK TO HER.

DEBBY AND HER FRIENDS FELT GOOD.

AND VERY SUPERIOR.

DEBBY AND KARYN AND BIANCA — THEY
WERE QUITE A GROUP.

TOP 3 GIRLS
DEBBY, KARYN
BIANCA

DEBBY WAS A HAPPY GIRL. SHE HAD A
NICE LIFE.

SPRINGSIDE
FOOTBALL

ALL CITY
TRACK
STEVE
UDISH
1979

HOWEVER, ONE DAY AT SCHOOL DEBBY
NOTICED SOMETHING. BUT MAYBE IT
WAS JUST HER IMAGINATION. . .

...KARYN AND BIANCA SEEMED TO BE EXCHANGING LOOKS.

AND THE LOOKS DIDN'T SEEM TO INCLUDE HER.

TWO DAYS LATER AT LUNCH, KAREN WAS TALKING TO BIANCA.

DEBBY DIDN'T KNOW WHAT THEY WERE TALKING ABOUT.

DEBBY REALIZED THAT KARYN AND BIANCA HAD BEEN TALKING ABOUT THINGS AND NOT INCLUDING HER.

MAYBE THEY WERE EVEN TALKING ABOUT HER.

THEN THE NEXT DAY IN SCHOOL, KARYN SPOKE SHARPLY TO HER.

DEBBY WAS VERY CONCERNED.

THEN THAT FRIDAY NIGHT THE WORST OF HER FEARS WERE REALIZED. KARYN AND BIANCA HAD BOTH SAID THEY HAD TO STAY HOME THAT NIGHT.

SO DEBBY WENT TO THE MOVIES WITH HER AUNT VAL, WHO LOVED MOVIES.

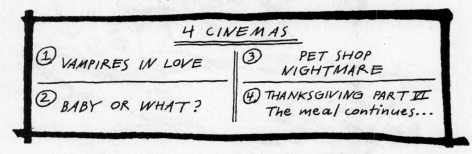

BUT AT THE MOVIES, IN THE FRONT ON THE LEFT, NO QUESTION ABOUT IT, WERE KARYN AND BIANCA AND RACHEL.

DEBBY WENT HOME, SHAKEN.

SHE COULD BARELY GET HERSELF TO GO
TO SCHOOL ON MONDAY. HAD SHE
BECOME -

UNPOPULAR

DID IT SHOW?

THE MORNING WENT OKAY, BUT SHE GOT
TO LUNCH EARLY AND HAD TO SIT ALONE
FOR A WHILE. THERE WAS AN EMPTY
SEAT RIGHT NEXT TO HER.

THEN, TO DEBBY'S TOTAL HORROR, BECKY PARKER CAME OVER AND ASKED IF SHE COULD SIT NEXT TO HER.

AND BEFORE DEBBY COULD SAY ANYTHING, SHE SAT DOWN. AND SHE STARTED TO TALK TO DEBBY.

DEBBY WAS IN A PANIC.

WHAT IF ANYBODY SAW HER WITH BECKY
PARKER?

WHAT COULD DEBBY DO?

DEBBY FLED. SHE SPENT THE REST OF
THE PERIOD HIDING IN THE GIRL'S ROOM.

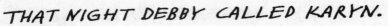

THAT NIGHT DEBBY CALLED KARYN.

WHY DON'T YOU AND BIANCA LIKE ME ANYMORE?

I DON'T KNOW WHAT YOU'RE TALKING ABOUT, DEBBY.

BUT DEBBY KNEW KARYN WAS LYING.

DEBBY GREW DESPERATE. SHE DECIDED TO COUNTERATTACK. THE FOLLOWING NIGHT SHE CALLED BIANCA.

I MEAN, I REALLY LIKE KARYN BUT I WAS SURPRISED WHEN CARLA TURSKY TOLD ME TODAY THAT KARYN HAD SAID TO HER THAT SHE THOUGHT YOU WERE A LITTLE STUCK-UP. HAVE YOU NOTICED THAT KARYN'S EYEBROWS ARE REAL CLOSE TOGETHER?

SHE ALSO CALLED UP KARYN.

JIMMY BISHOP TOLD ME THAT HE TOLD BIANCA THAT HE LIKES YOU, AND BIANCA SAID TO HIM, "I DON'T KNOW WHY." MAYBE HE MISUNDERSTOOD WHAT SHE SAID, AFTER ALL, BIANCA IS REALLY SO SWEET. HAVE YOU EVER NOTICED THE WAY SHE SOMETIMES HOLDS HER HEAD FUNNY?

BUT THE NEXT DAY IN SCHOOL KARYN AND BIANCA SEEMED AS TIGHT AS EVER.

YOU'VE BEEN WEARING THAT SWEATER A LOT LATELY, DEBBY, HAVEN'T YOU?

IS YOUR FAMILY HAVING TROUBLE WITH MONEY?

AND THEY WERE GETTING MEAN.

DEBBY STARTED DREADING GOING TO SCHOOL. SHE WOKE UP WORRYING EACH DAY.

I DON'T UNDERSTAND. WHY DON'T THEY LIKE ME ANYMORE?

MAYBE TODAY IT WILL BE OVER. MAYBE TODAY THEY'LL LIKE ME AGAIN.

BUT EACH DAY IT WAS THE SAME.

WHEN WAS IT GOING TO END? MAYBE DEBBY WOULD HAVE TO MAKE NEW FRIENDS.

ACTUALLY, IT DID END SOON. KARYN AND
BIANCA STARTED TO GET BORED WITH
RACHEL.

SO... SUDDENLY... ONE DAY... JUST LIKE THAT,

IT WAS BACK TO LIKE IT WAS BEFORE.

AND DEBBY DIDN'T UNDERSTAND WHY.

BUT REALLY SHE DIDN'T CARE. SHE WAS
JUST HAPPY TO HAVE IT BACK THE WAY
IT WAS.

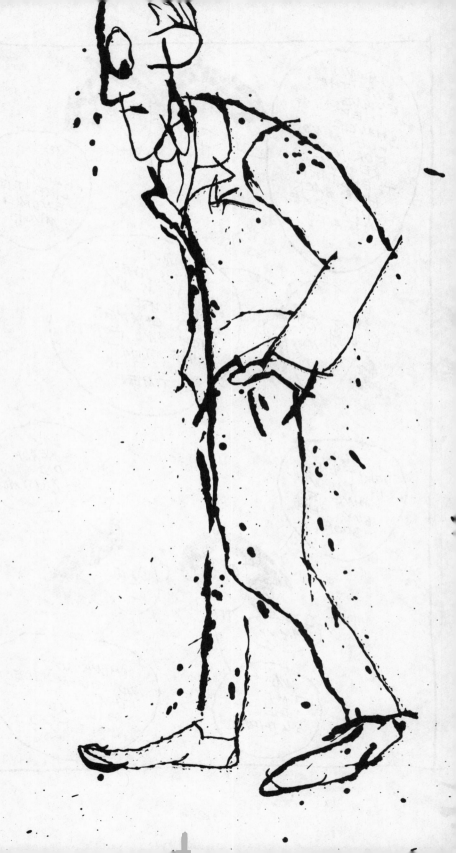

JUDITH'S PARENTS GET DIVORCED

Nobody likes his or her parents to get divorced. However, for teenagers, usually the biggest problems seem to come not from the upset and the sadness about the divorce itself, but from the many actual changes that take place in their lives following the break-up.

New issues come up: should one live with one's mother or father, increased financial strain within a two-household family, and, of course, being caught in the middle between one's own parents.

A particular problem with teenagers is adjusting to new step-parents. If a parent remarries when a child is still young, such as under six, a child can come to think of the step-parent as a parent—not replacing a father or mother, but as another father or mother. But with teenagers, there is no way they are going to view a new step-parent as a parent. The truth is that there are many situations where even when everything goes right, there will still be ongoing friction between child and step-parent. It really can be a no-win situation, and has to be accepted as that. Nice kids, nice step-parent—but they hate each other, at least while the children still live at home.

JUDITH USED TO WORRY ABOUT HER PARENTS GETTING DIVORCED.

BUT HER PARENTS NEVER DID SEEM TO GET ALONG THAT WELL.

JUDITH HAD HEARD OF CHILDREN WHOSE PARENTS HAD GOTTEN DIVORCED.

AND SHE HOPED IT WOULD NEVER HAPPEN TO HER.

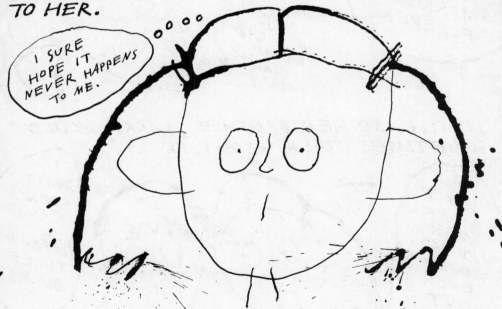

JUDITH CONTINUED TO WORRY.

BUT AT TIMES JUDITH WOULD GET SO AFRAID.
WHAT WOULD EVER HAPPEN IF THEY DID
GET DIVORCED?

YEARS WENT BY. JUDITH BECAME A
TEENAGER. SHE WORRIED A LITTLE LESS.
HER PARENTS WERE STILL TOGETHER.

MORE VERY HOT COFFEE, LIGHT OF MY LIFE?

BUT THEN ONE DAY THE UNTHINKABLE HAPPENED.

JUDITH'S WORLD EXPLODED INTO LITTLE PIECES.

JUDITH'S FATHER LEFT.

SHE AND LARRY STAYED WITH THEIR
MOTHER AND VISITED THEIR FATHER ON
WEEKENDS AND SOMETIMES DURING THE
WEEK.

STILL, JUDITH GRIEVED DESPERATELY.

BUT AS TIME PASSED, JUDITH BEGAN TO
NOTICE A FUNNY THING.

THE IDEA OF THE DIVORCE STILL MADE
HER FEEL SAD. BUT THE REALITY
WASN'T SO BAD.

HOWEVER, JUDITH DID NOT LIKE IT WHEN HER MOTHER AND FATHER WOULD TALK TO HER ABOUT EACH OTHER.

IT ALL MADE JUDITH FEEL VERY
UNCOMFORTABLE.

ON THE OTHER HAND SHE DID LIKE IT WHEN
HER PARENTS TRIED TO BUY HER
ALLEGIANCE.

BUT JUDITH DID HAVE NASTY DREAMS.

SOMETIMES JUDITH TRIED TO SHUT THEM UP.

AFTER A WHILE, THOUGH, JUDITH'S PARENTS'
FEUDING BECAME MORE OR LESS ROUTINE.

ACTUALLY, IT GOT TO BE THAT JUDITH WAS PRETTY CONTENT AND SHE HAD TROUBLE REMEMBERING WHAT IT HAD BEEN LIKE BEFORE.

BUT THEN ONE DAY A FUNNY THING HAPPENED.

MURRAY HAD BEEN DATING JUDITH'S MOTHER.
HE HAD SEVEN CHILDREN AND THEY ALL
MOVED IN.

IN TIME, JUDITH GOT USED TO THE CLOSET.

BUT SHE DID HAVE A LITTLE TROUBLE
ADJUSTING TO THE STRANGERS IN HER HOUSE.

YOU CAN'T COME IN HERE. IT'S OUR ROOM.
NO, IT'S MY ROOM! IT'S MY ROOM! IT WILL ALWAYS BE MY ROOM!
DADDY!

JUDITH FELT SHE HAD BEEN DISPLACED IN HER OWN HOME.

ALSO JUDITH DID NOT LIKE HER MOTHER'S RELATIONSHIP WITH MURRAY.

BUT JUDITH HAD ANOTHER SURPRISE, THIS TIME, FROM HER FATHER.

JUDITH, A MAN GETS LONELY. I'VE DECIDED TO MARRY LANA.

WHICH TURNED OUT NOT TO BE SO BAD BECAUSE LANA WAS SORT OF NEAR HER AGE AND THEY COULD DO STUFF TOGETHER.

DO YOU LIKE THIS APPLE MAUVE?

NOT REALLY. WHY DON'T YOU TRY MY FOREST AMBER?

MEANWHILE, MATTERS BETWEEN HER AND MURRAY WERE DETERIORATING. THEY BEGAN TO FIGHT CONSTANTLY.

THINGS WERE GETTING REALLY TENSE AND NASTY.

MATTERS WERE NOT GREAT BETWEEN JUDITH AND HER MOTHER, AND THEN ONE DAY:

THAT WAS TOO MUCH.

THAT EVENING JUDITH PACKED A SUITCASE AND WENT TO LIVE AT HER FATHER'S.

BUT AT HER FATHER'S THERE WAS A DEFINITE PROBLEM.

YOUR FATHER AND I HAVE BEEN THINKING THAT YOUR ALLOWANCE IS A LITTLE TOO HIGH.

WHAT!

LANA IS SPEAKING FOR BOTH OF US, DEAR.

AND A WEEK LATER:

DAD, CAN I GET MONEY FOR A NEW PAIR OF BOOTS? I REALLY NEED THEM.

YOUR FATHER AND I FEEL YOU HAVE TO LEARN TO ECONOMIZE ABOUT YOUR CLOTHES. YOU REALLY DO SPEND TOO MUCH.

LANA IS SPEAKING FOR BOTH OF US, DEAR.

JUDITH TALKED TO LARRY THE NEXT TIME HE CAME TO VISIT.

SHE STAYED A WEEK AT HER FRIEND CARLA'S.

JUDITH DECIDED TO RETURN TO HER MOTHER'S.

TO JUDITH'S SURPRISE, EVERYBODY AT HER MOTHER'S SEEMED HAPPY TO HAVE HER BACK, EVEN MURRAY.

ALSO, SHE GOT TO HAVE THE DOWNSTAIRS CLOSET, WHICH WAS SUBSTANTIALLY BIGGER THAN HER PREVIOUS CLOSET.

AND AS A MATTER OF FACT, AS TIME WENT BY THINGS REALLY WERE BETTER.

ME AND MURRAY FIGHT SOMETIMES. BUT IT'S NOT REALLY THAT BAD.

DISGUSTING, SPOILED SLUT!

TOTALLY LECHEROUS SLIME PERSON!

IT WAS NOT THAT SHE HAD GOTTEN TO LIKE MURRAY, IT WAS MORE THAT SHE HAD GOTTEN USED TO HIM.

I THINK I'M MORE MATURE. I JUST HAVE TO ACCEPT SOME THINGS.

JUDITH STILL SAW HER FATHER, BUT THEY WERE NOT AS CLOSE.

BUT OVERALL, JUDITH FELT SHE HAD
ADJUSTED TO HER PARENTS' DIVORCE.

I MEAN,
PARENTS GETTING
DIVORCED IS A TERRIBLE
THING AND ALL, BUT
I GUESS THERE ARE
WORSE THINGS
THAT COULD HAPPEN
TO A KID.

WE'RE NEVER
GOING TO GET DIVORCED
WHEN WE GROW UP, BECAUSE
WE'RE NEVER GOING TO GET
MARRIED. WE'RE GOING TO
BE ON TV.

CAROLINE AND HER BREASTS

Young teenage girls are generally concerned about pretty basic issues. "How am I doing in school? Am I popular? Are my parents mad at me?" These concerns are more than enough to occupy them. Hence the onset of adolescent body changes is often experienced as an intrusion: "I have enough trouble keeping my life in order, don't tell me I have to fuss about having a period and growing breasts."

Above all, what most young teenage girls want is to be liked and accepted by other girls their age. In this regard it is important not to be very different. Some girls develop physically before their friends. Though the friends may be envious—"Karen's a woman and I'm still a little girl"—the ones who are first to have breasts rarely enjoy it. They feel different, separate from their friends. In time their friends' bodies will develop, too, and they will all be together in the world of mature female bodies. But until then, the girls who develop first often wish they could go back to nice, comfortable, asexual prepubescence.

CAROLINE USED TO BE A LITTLE GIRL.

AND SHE HAD A LITTLE GIRL'S BODY. KIND OF LIKE A MATCH STICK.

SHE HAD NORMAL BREASTS—SORT OF LIKE LITTLE RAISINS STICKING OUT OF HER CHEST.

BUT THEN ONE DAY WHEN SHE WAS ELEVEN YEARS OLD, A FUNNY THING HAPPENED. HER BREASTS STARTED TO GROW—

(NOT TO MENTION CERTAIN OTHER LESS THAN THRILLING CHANGES).

WHAT MADE THINGS WORSE WAS THAT HER
BEST FRIEND LISA'S DIDN'T.

LISA'S BREASTS WERE STILL LIKE RAISINS
AND HER BODY WAS STILL LIKE A MATCH
STICK.

CAROLINE'S BREASTS CONTINUED TO GROW.

SHE WAS NOT PLEASED.

HER BREASTS DEFINITELY SHOWED, NO
MATTER WHAT TOPS SHE WORE.

SHE TOOK TO WEARING SWEATSHIRTS.

THEY HELPED A LITTLE. BUT AT HOME,
WHEN SHE CHANGED OR TOOK A
SHOWER, THEY WERE STILL THERE.

AND SHE FELT THEY WEREN'T HER
FRIENDS. SHE DIDN'T EVEN FEEL
THEY WERE PART OF HER BODY.

SHE OFTEN GAVE THEM NAMES.

CAROLINE DECIDED TO HAVE A POSITIVE
ATTITUDE ABOUT HER BREASTS. SO SHE
GAVE THEM NICE NAMES AFTER HER
RECENTLY DEAD GERBILS.

SHE WAS FEELING A LITTLE BETTER
ABOUT HER BREASTS.

HOWEVER, ONE DAY IN SCHOOL, BUTCH THUNGMAN, WHO WAS THE TOUGHEST KID IN THE SCHOOL, CAME UP TO CAROLINE AND SAID,

HEY, YOU'VE GOT BIG TITS.

THAT DID IT. THE NEXT DAY CAROLINE CARRIED A TABLE TO SCHOOL.

AND SHE WOULD NOT PUT IT DOWN, EVEN IN CLASS.

CAROLINE'S TEACHER, MRS. PRIDDY, ASKED HER:

WHY ARE YOU HOLDING THAT TABLE?

CAROLINE ANSWERED,

THIS IS A TABLE AND MY BREASTS ARE TINY JUST LIKE LITTLE RAISINS, A FACT WHICH YOU COULD SEE IF I PUT DOWN THIS TABLE, WHICH I WON'T.

CAROLINE CONTINUED TO BRING THE TABLE TO SCHOOL.

SOME OF THE KIDS STARTED TO TEASE HER.

IS THAT YOUR NEW BOYFRIEND?

WANT SOME FURNITURE POLISH? HAR! HAR! HAR!

BUT CAROLINE DIDN'T CARE.

THEY'RE JUST JEALOUS.

CAROLINE'S PARENTS BECAME CONCERNED.

THEY DECIDED TO SPEAK TO CAROLINE.

CAROLINE'S PARENTS DISCUSSED THE MATTER.

THEY DECIDED TO GET PROFESSIONAL HELP.

DR. E.J. SNARKLER

CHILDREN AND FAMILIES

DR. SNARKLER WAS A WARM AND WONDERFUL MAN WHO ESPECIALLY LOVED CHILDREN AND SMALL ANIMALS.

CAROLINE'S PARENTS TOOK HER TO SEE HIM.

DR. SNARKLER MADE SOME RECOMMENDATIONS TO CAROLINE'S PARENTS.

CAROLINE'S PARENTS WEREN'T SURE WHAT THEY THOUGHT.

THEY DECIDED TO TRY DR. SNARKLER'S RECOMMENDATIONS.

BUT THE ONLY THING THAT HAPPENED WAS THAT CAROLINE GOT TO LIKE CARROT JUICE A LITTLE.

SHE STILL BROUGHT THE TABLE TO SCHOOL.

POMEROY L. KINSWORTHY
JUNIOR HIGH SCHOOL

CAROLINE'S PARENTS GAVE UP AND DROPPED THE PUNISHMENTS..

AFTER A WHILE PEOPLE AT SCHOOL BEGAN
TO ACCEPT CAROLINE'S TABLE.

STILL, SHE DIDN'T LIKE HER BREASTS TOO
MUCH.

BUT THEY WEREN'T THAT BAD.

ALSO, HER OTHER BEST FRIEND, JANIS,
BEGAN CARRYING THE COLLECTED WORKS
OF BJÖRN KVÖLDSEN AROUND WITH
HER ALL THE TIME.

THEN ONE DAY CAROLINE HURT HER ARM WHILE HITTING HER LITTLE BROTHER, KEVIN.

AND THE NEXT DAY. HER ARM STILL HURT.

WHICH MADE IT HARD TO CARRY THE
TABLE TO SCHOOL.

SO SHE DIDN'T. AND SHE NEVER DID AGAIN.

THE
TABLE WAS
REALLY PRETTY
HEAVY.

HER PARENTS WERE PLEASED, THOUGH
NOT VERY.

I'D
KIND OF
GOTTEN
USED
TO IT.

IT
WAS SO
GOOD
FOR HER
POSTURE.

HER FRIENDS DIDN'T REALLY SEEM TO NOTICE.

ONE DAY IN SCHOOL BUTCH THUNGMAN SAID TO CAROLINE,

CAROLINE JUST SMILED...

THEY WERE KIND OF BIG, BUT THEY WEREN'T THAT BIG.

MANY YEARS LATER, WHEN CAROLINE WAS
TWENTY-SIX, SHE WAS TALKING WITH
HER MOTHER. AND SHE SAID,

DO YOU REMEMBER WHEN YOU CARRIED A TABLE TO SCHOOL FOR ALL THAT TIME?

CAROLINE WAS SURPRISED. SHE DID SORT
OF REMEMBER DOING SOMETHING LIKE
THAT. BUT SHE COULDN'T FOR THE
LIFE OF HER REMEMBER WHY.

THE WORRIES OF JAMES' MOTHER

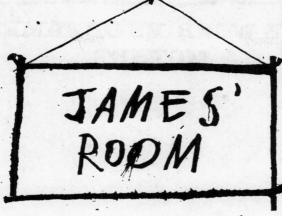

JAMES'
ROOM

GIVE ME
LIBERTY OR
GIVE ME
CINDY APPLETON
NAKED

MEGA
MAIM

THE WORRIES OF JAMES' MOTHER

With adolescence, teenage girls can turn into monsters. Most teenage boys, however, turn into something quite different. And this, for some parents, can be even harder to take than a monster in the house, harder because it involves a real loss. This often happens between mothers and sons.

What was once a bright, bubbly, talkative, and loving son disappears. What was once a boy who was his mother's little companion and hug-a-bunny becomes someone unavailable, aloof, someone who seems to broadcast that his mother's very presence in the room makes him uncomfortable—which it actually does.

It can happen with fathers, too, but more often with mothers. What used to be a special intimacy often vanishes with adolescence.

Why does this happen? First, because of a boy's need in adolescence to establish his own independence. But also a boy's newly emergent sexual feelings, and the fact that his mother is a woman, make for a certain amount of discomfort for him. This does not last forever. Hopefully, by the end of adolescence, the necessary distance is achieved. The boy, now a young man with an adequate sense of his own maturity and manhood, can return to being nice and friendly again. It is all rather bewildering to the parent who has to go through it. It can be confusing, too, to the boy who does not really understand why the less he has to do with his parents, the better he feels.

ON THE DAY HE TURNED FOURTEEN,
JAMES WENT INTO HIS ROOM, CLOSED
THE DOOR, AND DIDN'T COME OUT
EXCEPT TO EAT SUPPER OR LEAVE
THE HOUSE.

HIS PARENTS WEREN'T TOO CONCERNED.
BUT AFTER A WHILE:

WHEN THEY DID SEE HIM AT SUPPER, HE WAS NOT VERY COMMUNICATIVE.

JAMES' PARENTS WONDERED...

THE SOUND OF HIS STEREO WAS ALWAYS COMING FROM JAMES' ROOM. THEY ASKED JAMES...

...BUT LEARNED LITTLE.

THERE WAS ANOTHER THING. JAMES
SEEMED TO HAVE SLEEPING SICKNESS.
BUT ONLY AT HOME. JAMES NOTICED IT
TOO.

FOR EXAMPLE, ONE TIME JAMES WAS
SITTING IN THE FAMILY ROOM (A RARE
OCCURRENCE) AND THERE WAS AN EMPTY
GLASS ON A TABLE NEAR HIM.

HIS FATHER ASKED IF HE WOULD TAKE THE
GLASS INTO THE KITCHEN.

JAMES NOTICED A FUNNY THING. SUDDENLY
HE WAS TERRIBLY TIRED AND EVEN
MOVING SEEMED BEYOND HIS CAPABILITY.

HE TRIED. HE REALLY HAD NOTHING AGAINST
TAKING THE GLASS INTO THE KITCHEN. BUT
HE WAS SO TIRED. IT SEEMED LIKE SUCH
AN EFFORT.

IT WAS ALL JAMES COULD DO TO LIFT
HIMSELF OUT OF THE CHAIR AND STUMBLE
INTO HIS ROOM AND CLOSE THE DOOR.

JAMES WAS ALWAYS COOPERATIVE.

HE JUST NEVER SEEMED TO GET AROUND TO DOING ANYTHING.

BESIDES THE SLEEPING SICKNESS, JAMES SEEMED TO DEVELOP SOME OTHER SYMPTOMS. HE DIDN'T LIKE TO BE TOUCHED.

EVEN SLIGHTLY.

IT'S THE MIDDLE OF THE AFTERNOON, WHY IS JAMES TAKING A SHOWER?

I THINK IT'S BECAUSE I BRUSHED AGAINST HIS ARM IN THE HALL.

AT LEAST BY HIS PARENTS.

HE DID SPEND A LOT OF TIME IN THE SHOWER.

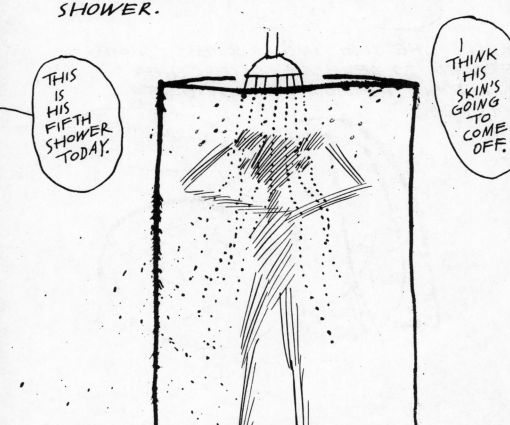

THIS IS HIS FIFTH SHOWER TODAY.

I THINK HIS SKIN'S GOING TO COME OFF.

JAMES' SCHOOLWORK WAS A MYSTERY. HE NEVER SEEMED TO STUDY.

YET HE GOT B'S AND C'S ON HIS REPORT CARD.

AT HOME, ALL JAMES SEEMED TO DO WAS HANG OUT IN HIS ROOM LISTENING TO MUSIC.

JAMES' MOTHER REALLY BEGAN TO WORRY.

SHE TRIED TALKING TO HIM. BUT HE WAS ALWAYS SO HARD TO CATCH.

ONE DAY JAMES HAD A FRIEND OVER.

.THEY SPENT THE EVENING IN JAMES' ROOM.

SHE WORRIED MORE.

TWO WEEKS LATER, A PACKAGE CAME FOR JAMES. JAMES' MOTHER COULDN'T HELP BUT OPEN IT.

JAMES' MOTHER WAS SHOCKED BY THE PACKAGE'S CONTENTS.

SHE SHOWED THE BOOK TO JAMES' FATHER.

JAMES' MOTHER BECAME OBSESSED.

WHAT IS HAPPENING TO HIM? I HAVE TO KNOW WHAT IS GOING ON WITH HIM. HIS WHOLE FUTURE IS AT STAKE.

SHE HIRED A DETECTIVE.

AFTER A MONTH, THE DETECTIVE
REPORTED BACK TO HER.

JAMES' MOTHER WAS NOT SATISFIED AT
ALL.

WORRYING ABOUT JAMES FILLED HER
EVERY MOMENT.

HE'S GOING
TO GROW UP
TO BE A
SADIST.

HE'S GOING
TO BE A BUM.

HE'LL JOIN A
CIRCUS AND DIE
A DOPE FIEND.

HE'LL
NEVER HOLD
HIS FORK
RIGHT.

TIME WENT BY AND NOTHING MUCH
CHANGED. OCCASIONALLY, JAMES'
MOTHER TRIED AGAIN TO OPEN UP
COMMUNICATION...

TALK TO
ME OR I'LL
KILL YOU.
I MEAN
IT.

MOM,
YOU'RE
MESSING UP
MY HAIR.

... BUT WITH LITTLE SUCCESS.

JAMES' MOTHER DECIDED THAT SHE
WOULD TAKE UP FULL-CONTACT
KARATE TO HELP KEEP HER MIND
OFF WORRYING ABOUT JAMES.

IT HELPED SOME.

MORE TIME WENT BY. IT GOT TO BE
JAMES' SENIOR YEAR IN HIGH SCHOOL.

THEN ONE DAY, IN DECEMBER, JAMES
CAME TO HIS PARENTS.

WHICH IS WHAT HE DID.

AND JAMES' MOTHER DIDN'T WORRY ABOUT HIM ANYMORE. SHE WORRIED ABOUT OTHER THINGS:

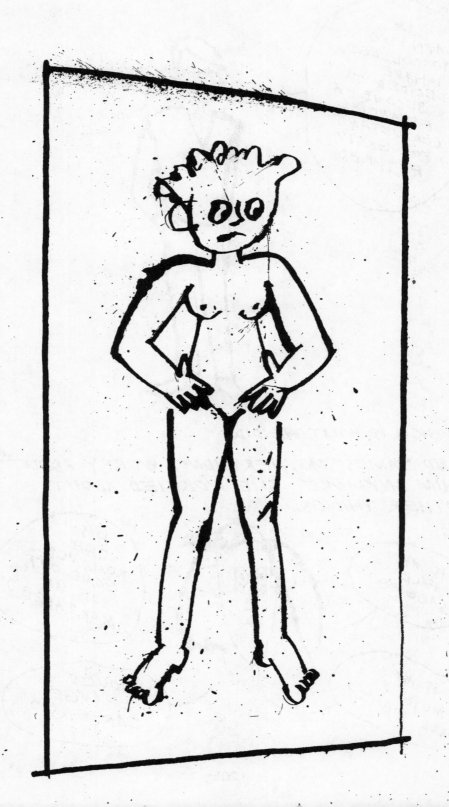

THE GIRL WHO THOUGHT SHE WAS JUST A LITTLE TOO FAT

THE GIRL WHO THOUGHT
SHE WAS JUST A LITTLE TOO FAT

I heard of a study which claimed that half of the fourth-grade girls in the United States were on a diet. That's crazy. Superconsciousness of how women are supposed to look is everywhere—TV, ads, fashion magazines—and the correct look is thin. Somehow, in adolescence a sense of "I never quite look good enough" combines with newly emergent sexual feelings and becomes more than many girls can handle.

Sexuality for teenage girls—which is very different from that for teenage boys—has a lot to do with feeling attractive, beautiful. And for many teenage girls that translates into not feeling attractive, beautiful enough. The problem is that all too easily this can get way out of hand. Girls can get some pretty strange ideas about how they look and how they should look.

Anorexia nervosa is the extreme version of this. Girls truly believe that their wafer-thin bodies still could be a little thinner, a little more perfect. But most teenage girls with perfectly nice bodies also believe that they are too fat. It is a real problem. And, of course, it doesn't end with the teenage years.

WHEN MARISSA WAS EIGHT YEARS OLD, HER
PARENTS GAVE HER A SHAWNA DOLL.

RIGHT AWAY, MARISSA LOVED SHAWNA. SHE
WAS SO BEAUTIFUL. SO PERFECT. SO TINY.

MARISSA WANTED TO GROW UP TO LOOK JUST
LIKE SHAWNA. SHE WAS SO BEAUTIFUL.
AND MARISSA LOVED HER SO MUCH.

AND MARISSA KNEW THAT SHAWNA LOVED HER TOO.

DON'T YOU, SHAWNA?

BUT SHAWNA NEVER ANSWERED. SHE JUST SMILED AND LOOKED BEAUTIFUL AND PERFECT. LIKE SHE ALWAYS DID.

BUT, ONE DAY, A FUNNY THING HAPPENED. MARISSA COULD REMEMBER THE DAY CLEARLY. SHE WAS NINE YEARS OLD. SHE HAD BEEN WATCHING "KEEP SLIM WITH SARA JEAN" ON TV,

WHILE LEAFING THROUGH AN ISSUE OF
MISS BOUTIQUE MAGAZINE.

WHAT HAPPENED WAS THAT SHAWNA SPOKE
TO HER.

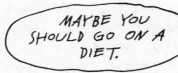

MARISSA WAS VERY EXCITED.

SHE WANTED TO DO WHAT SHAWNA SAID.

SO THAT NIGHT AT SUPPER, ON PURPOSE, MARISSA DID NOT EAT HER FRENCH FRIES.

MARISSA WAS VERY PLEASED WITH HER WILL POWER. AND SHAWNA WAS PLEASED, TOO.

THAT WAS EXCELLENT, DEAR.

FROM THEN ON SHAWNA WAS MARISSA'S FRIEND AND TALKED TO HER EVERY DAY.

HONEYBUMPKINS, YOU'RE PERFECT, YOU REALLY ARE. BUT MAYBE YOU HAVE A TEENSY WEENSY TOO MUCH TUMMY.

ALWAYS, SHAWNA LIKED TO TALK ABOUT BEING THIN.

TREASURE LAMB, DO YOU REALLY WANT TO PUT SUGAR ON YOUR CEREAL?

MARISSA LOVED SHAWNA. SHE WANTED TO PLEASE HER. AND MARISSA DID LIKE THE IDEA OF BEING THIN.

AFTER ALL, MARISSA DID WANT TO GROW
UP TO BE A BEAUTIFUL WOMAN.

WHICH SHE KNEW MEANT THIN. SO
MARISSA DIETED. A LITTLE.

YEARS PASSED. MARISSA BECAME A TEENAGER.
AND SHE STARTED TO HAVE DISTURBING
DREAMS.

THE DREAMS WERE ALWAYS ABOUT HER
BEING IN THE MOVIES.

MARISSA TOWLER IN
THE RETURN OF THE HIPPO PEOPLE

THE ATTACK OF THE ELEPHANT WOMEN
STARRING MARISSA TOWLER

MELISSA TOWLER IS WHALE WOMAN

STILL, MARISSA DECIDED THAT SHE WAS TOO FAT.

GOOD FOR YOU.

I NEED TO GO ON A SERIOUS DIET.

SO MARISSA LOST WEIGHT. BUT IT WASN'T ENOUGH.

I HAVE TO GET THINNER FOR THE SUMMER.

YOU'LL BULGE IN A BIKINI.

SHE LOST A LOT OF WEIGHT. MARISSA
WAS PLEASED. ALMOST.

MARISSA DID WANT TO BE PERFECT SO SHE
DIETED SOME MORE.

MARISSA WAS VERY HAPPY. ESPECIALLY WITH
SHAWNA'S NEW SUGGESTION.

MARISSA GOT THINNER AND THINNER AND PROUDER AND HAPPIER.

MARISSA'S FRIENDS WERE NOT SO SURE.

BOYS WERE NOT EXACTLY TURNED ON.

SUMMER CAME AND MARISSA WAS THE THINNEST GIRL ON THE BEACH.

MARISSA'S PARENTS WERE CONCERNED ALSO.

BUT MARISSA KNEW THEY WERE ONLY JEALOUS.

SHE BECAME FAMOUS.

MARISSA FELT SHE NOW HAD ALMOST A PERFECT FIGURE. BUT SHE COULD STILL PINCH HER TUMMY.

SO SHE DIETED MORE.

THEN ONE DAY, AS MARISSA WAS WALKING TO SCHOOL, A GUST OF WIND CAME ALONG AND PICKED HER UP AND CARRIED HER HIGH INTO THE SKY.

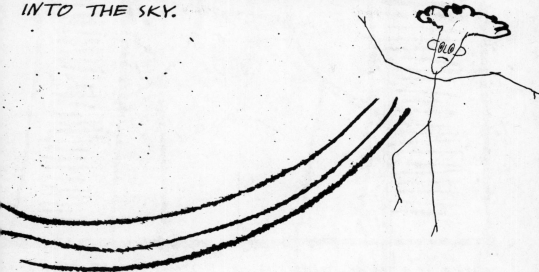

THE WIND CARRIED MARISSA ALL THE WAY TO THE HAPPY VIEW FARMS SANITARIUM.

AND THERE SHE STAYED.

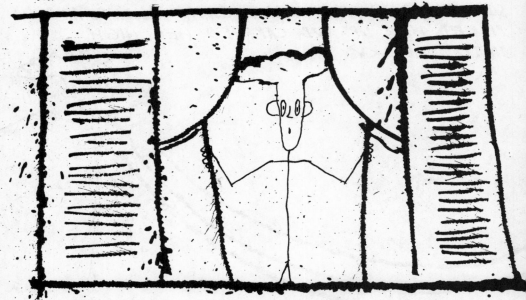

MARISSA WAS THERE A LONG, LONG TIME.
FINALLY, AFTER MANY, MANY TALKS
WITH HER DOCTORS AND WITH HER
NEW FRIEND, RENEE, WHO WAS VERY
THIN JUST LIKE HER — MARISSA
CHANGED.

YOU KNOW, MAYBE I AM JUST A BIT TOO THIN.

MARISSA DECIDED THAT SHE HAD TO HAVE A
TALK WITH SHAWNA. AND SHE HAD HER
PARENTS BRING SHAWNA THE NEXT
VISITING DAY.

GOSH, SHAWNA, THE DOCTORS SAY I COULD DIE BECAUSE I'M SO THIN. AND I DO WEIGH LESS THAN MOST FIVE-YEAR-OLD GIRLS. AND I REALLY DON'T LOOK LIKE ANY OF MY FRIENDS.

BUT SHAWNA WOULD NOT UNDERSTAND. SHE
WAS FURIOUS.

YOU'LL BE DISGUSTING. GROSS. YUCCH! YUCCH! YUCCH!

SO MARISSA HAD TO DECIDE ON HER OWN. AND SHE DECIDED THAT MAYBE SHAWNA WAS A BIT OF A NUT CASE. MARISSA STARTED TO EAT NORMALLY AGAIN.

A WHILE LATER, WHEN MARISSA CAME HOME FROM THE HOSPITAL, SHE FOUND THAT SHE DIDN'T HAVE THE HEART TO THROW SHAWNA AWAY. SO MARISSA PUT HER IN A CORNER OF THE STORAGE ROOM IN THE BASEMENT. AND THERE SHAWNA RAVED ON.

OH YOU'RE SO DISGUSTING. MISS FATTY GROSSBODY THAT'S WHO YOU ARE. PLUMPELLA TONPOUNDS, THAT'S WHAT THEY'LL CALL YOU. PLEASE, AT LEAST DRINK DIET SODA. LETTUCE WON'T HURT YOU...

BUT MARISSA COULDN'T HEAR HER.

EVELYN AND HER PARENTS

The main psychological fact of adolescence is that teenagers develop an absolute need to stop being children, especially in relation to their parents. For themselves, they *have* to get a sense of their own independence. Because of this, suddenly a parent's very presence becomes a great strain. If the parents speak or—even worse—give orders, it borders on the intolerable. This is so because teenagers, whether they like it or not, still have strong emotional ties to their parents. And these ties are in direct conflict with their need to be independent. Boys and girls tend to go through adolescence differently. Boys tend to disappear. "Jerry, will you take out the trash?" "Sure," says Jerry as he leaves the room, not to be seen for a couple of days. Boys get their independence by being distant.

Girls hang right in there. They establish their independence by doing and saying the opposite. "Sharon, take out the trash." "Why me?" Girls are ready to do battle. I think that the girls' method may be better—if their parents don't kill them or themselves. Boys, by isolating, cut themselves off from their parents and are forced to deal with their problems very much on their own, which is hard. Teenage girls definitely have more of a relationship with their parents, however stormy, than do boys. And so it ends up that they don't have to shoulder quite as many of the burdens of adolescence all on their own. This is probably a major reason why far more teenage boys than girls kill themselves (apart from the fact that boys use more effective methods—guns, ropes, and car exhaust).

EVELYN HAD ALWAYS BEEN A NICE AND
COOPERATIVE LITTLE GIRL. HER PARENTS
HAD OFTEN CALLED HER "OUR LITTLE
ANGEL."

SHE REALLY HAD BEEN.

SHE WAS FRIENDLY AND NICE AND HAD A
SENSE OF HUMOR, AND WHEN YOU ASKED HER
TO DO SOMETHING, SHE DID IT.

EVELYN, WOULD YOU HELP ME WITH THIS LAUNDRY?

SURE, MOM.

EVELYN, WOULD YOU SLICE THE ZUCCHINI FOR ME?

SURE, DAD.

SHE WAS JUST A NICE LITTLE GIRL. AND
HER PARENTS LOVED HER.

THEN ONE DAY, WHEN EVELYN WAS IN
THE SEVENTH GRADE, JANUARY
THIRTEENTH, TO BE EXACT, SHE
CHANGED.

AND SHE WASN'T NICE ANYMORE.

EVELYN'S MOTHER FIRST NOTICED IT THAT EVENING.

EVELYN, WOULD YOU PUT THE DISHES IN THE DISHWASHER?

WHAT?

NO.

EVELYN'S FATHER DIDN'T NOTICE IT UNTIL THE NEXT EVENING.

EVELYN, WOULD YOU HELP ME SLICE THE ZUCCHINI?

WHAT?

WHY DON'T YOU ASK LARRY?

I SAID, WHY DON'T YOU ASK LARRY? HE'S NOT DOING ANYTHING.

EVELYN'S FATHER WAS PUZZLED.

BECAUSE I'M ASKING YOU.

YOU NEVER MAKE LARRY DO STUFF.

EVELYN GOT UPSET. AND SHE RAN CRYING UP TO HER ROOM.

YOU DON'T HAVE TO YELL. YOU NEVER MAKE LARRY DO ANYTHING. YOU DON'T. I HATE YOU! I HATE YOU!

EVELYN'S FATHER WAS CONFUSED.

WHAT HAPPENED?

ALSO, THE ZUCCHINIS WERE LEFT UNSLICED.

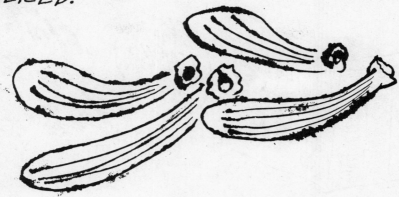

THINGS DID NOT GET BETTER. EVELYN BECAME MOODY.

AND GETTING HER TO DO ANYTHING BECAME A CONSTANT BATTLE.

I SAID, PICK UP THAT GLASS.

I'LL SEE YOU IN HELL FIRST!

EVELYN ALSO BECAME VERY SENSITIVE.

ESPECIALLY ABOUT HOW SHE LOOKED.

THEN ONE DAY THEY HAD A BIG CRISIS.

EVELYN REFUSED TO GO TO SCHOOL.

I CAN'T GO.

EVELYN'S MOTHER TRIED TO REASON WITH HER.

BUT YOU HAVE SIX OTHER PERFECTLY NICE SWEATERS.

IT DIDN'T WORK.

SHE FLATLY REFUSED TO GO.

EVELYN'S PARENTS TRIED.

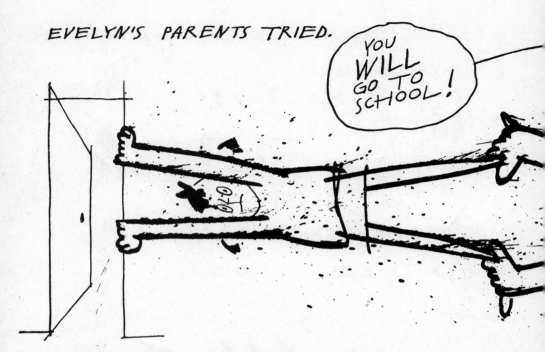

BUT IN THE END, THEY COULDN'T FORCE HER AND EVELYN DID STAY HOME.

THE NEXT DAY THE SWEATER WAS BACK
FROM THE CLEANERS AND EVELYN
WENT TO SCHOOL.

BUT THE BATTLES BECAME EVEN UGLIER.

YOU'RE A COMPLETELY UNGRATEFUL GIRL AND I'M ASHAMED TO HAVE YOU FOR A DAUGHTER.

YOU WISH THE MISCARRIAGE YOU HAD BETWEEN ME AND LARRY HAD LIVED AND I HAD DIED.

AND A FUNNY THING WAS THAT A LITTLE
WHILE AFTER EACH OF THESE BATTLES,
EVELYN SEEMED IN A PERFECTLY
GOOD MOOD.

EVELYN'S PARENTS DECIDED THEY HAD TO DO SOMETHING.

THEY TRIED LECTURES.

DON'T YOU UNDERSTAND THAT YOUR MOTHER AND I ONLY WANT WHAT'S BEST FOR YOU AND THAT ALL WE ASK IN RETURN IS THAT YOU COOPERATE AT HOME WHEN WE ASK YOU TO....

THEY TRIED GETTING TO THE ROOT OF
THE PROBLEM.

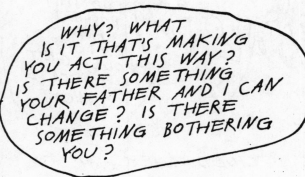 

WHY? WHAT
IS IT THAT'S MAKING
YOU ACT THIS WAY?
IS THERE SOMETHING
YOUR FATHER AND I CAN
CHANGE? IS THERE
SOMETHING BOTHERING
YOU?

WILL
YOU GET
OFF MY
BACK?

THEY TRIED PUNISHMENT.

UNTIL
YOU CAN
LEARN TO
BEHAVE,
YOU'RE
GROUNDED
FOR A
MONTH.

WHY
DON'T
YOU
JUST
DIE.

THAT WAS A DISASTER. BECAUSE SHE WAS
AROUND THE HOUSE MORE, THEY ONLY
FOUGHT MORE.

THEY TRIED CUTTING OFF HER PHONE.

BUT I HAVE TO CALL CLARISSA.

THAT WORKED. UNFORTUNATELY, DEPRIVED OF THE PHONE, EVELYN RAPIDLY BEGAN WASTING AWAY.

I'M AFRAID SHE'S DYING.

SO THEY HAD TO DISCONTINUE THAT PUNISHMENT.

HELLO, CLARISSA. DOES ROBBY STILL LIKE SUSAN?

ODDLY, SOME THINGS WERE NOT SO BAD.
EVELYN USUALLY DID HER HOMEWORK.

BUT SHE DID KEEP UP.

ALSO, THEY GOT STRANGE REPORTS FROM
OTHER PEOPLE EVELYN WOULD SPEND
TIME WITH.

ABOVE ALL, THERE WAS SOMETHING THAT
BOTHERED EVELYN'S MOTHER THE MOST.

IT JUST SO HAPPENED THAT IN THE TOWN
WHERE THEY LIVED THERE WAS AN
ORACLE. IT MYSTERIOUSLY SPOKE
THROUGH A SPEAKER AT AN ABANDONED
DRIVE-IN MOVIE THEATER.

THE PECULIAR THING ABOUT THE ORACLE WAS THAT IT DID NOT ANSWER QUESTIONS IN STRANGE WAYS THAT NOBODY COULD UNDERSTAND, LIKE:

WHAT YOU SEEK SHALL BE WHAT YOU SOUGHT.

THIS ORACLE WAS VERY SPECIFIC, AND IT WAS ALWAYS RIGHT. AND BECAUSE OF THIS NOT TOO MANY PEOPLE WENT TO IT.

I MEAN, WHO WANTS TO HEAR THAT YOU'RE GOING TO GET CANCER?

BUT EVELYN'S MOTHER WAS DESPERATE. SO SHE WENT TO THE ORACLE.

I'VE SIMPLY GOT TO KNOW.

MY DAUGHTER IS SPOILED AND UNGRATEFUL AND NASTY AND WE HAVE NO CONTROL OVER HER. WHAT'S GOING TO HAPPEN TO HER?

THE ORACLE ANSWERED.

YOUR DAUGHTER WILL GROW UP TO BE AN ACCOUNTANT, WILL MARRY AN ACCOUNTANT, AND WILL HAVE TWO CHILDREN, DONNY AND DAWN. SHE WILL BE A RESPECTED MEMBER OF HER COMMUNITY AND A KEY MEMBER OF HER LOCAL PTA. SHE WILL GET DIVORCED AFTER TWENTY-THREE YEARS OF MARRIAGE. WHEN HER DAUGHTER IS FIFTEEN, SHE WILL SAY TO HER THAT SHE IS SELFISH AND UNGRATEFUL AND THAT SHE DOES NOT UNDERSTAND HOW SHE COULD HAVE GOTTEN TO BE THE WAY SHE IS. SHE WILL DIE AT THE AGE OF SEVENTY-EIGHT OF HEART FAILURE FOLLOWING COMPLICATIONS FROM A BROKEN HIP.

EVELYN'S MOTHER WAS RELIEVED.

JOYFULLY, EVELYN'S MOTHER TOLD THE GOOD NEWS TO EVELYN'S FATHER.

EVELYN'S FATHER WAS NOT SO SURE. AND CERTAINLY EVELYN SHOWED NO SIGNS OF CHANGING.

EVELYN'S MOTHER KEPT GOING BACK TO THE ORACLE.

ARE YOU ABSOLUTELY SURE?

AND THE ORACLE KEPT SAYING THE SAME THING.

YOUR DAUGHTER WILL GROW UP TO BE AN ACCOUNTANT, WILL MARRY AN ACCOUNTANT...

SHE DID KEEP RETURNING TO THE ORACLE.

YOU NEVER UNDERSTAND ME!

THE ORACLE HAS NEVER BEEN WRONG.

NONETHELESS, EVELYN'S FATHER DECIDED TO RETIRE TO HIS WORKROOM IN THE BASEMENT.

I NEED $87.00 FOR A PAIR OF BOOTS.

ALBERT?

TIME WENT BY WITHOUT MUCH CHANGE.
AND THEN ONE DAY...

IT WAS APRIL 17 OF HER JUNIOR YEAR
IN HIGH SCHOOL, TO BE EXACT. EVELYN
CHANGED AGAIN.

AND IT WAS OVER AND THEY HAD THEIR
NICE EVELYN BACK.

AND EVELYN'S PARENTS WERE VERY HAPPY.

AND THEY LIVED HAPPILY EVER AFTER.

BUT WHAT THE ORACLE DIDN'T SAY WAS
THAT EVELYN'S CHILDREN VERY MUCH
ENJOYED THE EXACT REPLICA OF NEW
YORK CITY MADE FROM WATERMELON
SEEDS THAT EVELYN'S FATHER HAD MADE
DURING HIS TIME DOWNSTAIRS IN HIS
WORKROOM.

CONCLUSION

Why is it that people seem to remember their teenage
years with a certain poignancy? What is so special about
that time? In going through it, this period often seems
anything but special. But when you look back, somehow,
almost regardless of what actually went on, adolescence
takes on a brightness, an intensity, that seems un-
matched in the rest of one's life. It's not that it's a
happier time, it's just that the events seem larger than
life. A particular trip to the beach with friends was
somehow especially memorable. Yet, thinking back, there
were other, later beach outings, which were not so
different.

Childhood is childhood, and as we look back on it, we
remember it more as an outside observer would. But

adolescence is the beginning of our adult life: only then do we view the world with the same eyes and intelligence (particularly regarding sexuality) that we use for the rest of our lives.

Perhaps it is because these experiences *are* all new that events at this time shine so vividly later on. In adolescence everything *is* more poignant, and more traumatic.

We can't recapture our adolescence: it is not possible to go through things for the first time again. And if we're honest with ourselves we might ask: would we really want to?

Tony Wolf is a practicing clinical psychologist who has been seeing children and adolescents for sixteen years. He grew up in Philadelphia and went to school in New York City, where he received his undergraduate degree from Columbia and his Ph.D. from the City University of New York. For the last sixteen years he has lived in Massachusetts with his wife and two now teenage children. He is very fond of his wife and children. He is also inordinately fond of food. "I've never met a meatloaf I didn't like," he has often commented.

France Menk was born with a silver pen in her hand and has been drawing ever since. She is an ex-teenager, an ex-Outward Bound Instructor, and a step-mother. She has lived and worked in Spain, Britain, and Australia as a political cartoonist and photographer. Since returning to the United States in 1979, she has worked as an illustrator, graphic designer, and art director. She continues to use the same silver pen.